Preface: The Princess & Dragon Story

This collection of stories has a very

special meaning. It takes me back to

the early days of being a father with a

beautiful little girl sitting on my knee for story time.

Like all little girls, she loved stories about princesses

and dragons. She still does! This volume is dedicated

to her.

Of course, this collection isn't just for girls!

There are plenty of dragons, knights and other

adventures that boys will love. I know first-hand

because my boys (6 and 10) loved reading every story

before they were published.

It seems there is nothing more treasured in literature than the princess and dragon story. Why? Because children love adventure and danger, heroes and heroines, and of course, happy endings. Every story, every word, every adventure, every daring rescue, every lesson learned — it's all new and exciting to children.

Through these stories, they explore the world around them. They learn about good vs. evil, about friendship and love, about right and wrong, about choices and consequences and so much more.

And all the while, their inquisitive minds are learning new vocabulary, improving listening and reading skills, and literally being hard-wired to learn

- preparing them to become successful in school and

in life.

   There is no better early childhood development

program than when a parent takes the time to sit

down and read with a child every day. To that end,

we offer you this special collection of timeless

princess and dragon stories in the hope that both you

and your child will love the experience of joining in

the adventures and excitement together.

Phillip J. Chipping // Founder
knowonder! publishing
www.knowonder.com

About DyslexiAssist™

Part of our mission at Knowonder! Publishing is to make literacy more effective. In order to fulfill that mission for children suffering from dyslexia we are proud to announce our new DyslexiAssist™ initiative: to publish each of our books in a special font designed to make reading easier for dyslexics. You can learn more about it on our website at:

www.knowonder.com/dyslexiassist

When reading with this new font, independent research shows that 84% of dyslexics read faster, 77% read with fewer mistakes, and 76% recommend the font to others who suffer from dyslexia.

But the magic isn't just in the font. We take

extra care to make the font an appropriate size, give

proper spacing to letters in the words, make sure that

there are the exact right number of words on each

line, and so much more! The layout of the book is just

as important. We go to extra lengths to make sure

all the stars are aligned so they, too, can know the

wonder of reading.

Reading stories is a highly enjoyable form of

entertainment but people with dyslexia have been

unable to find the same joy from books. We hope this

new initiative can now bring the same love and joy of

reading and learning to your home!

Table of Contents

A collection

of princess and dragon stories

(perfect for bedtime!)

for children ages 0-12

and for parents

who want to feel like a kid again.

- Volume 2 -

ISBN: 978-1517046132

Dedicated to my princess,
my "darling angel baby doll."
I love you forever!

The Ice Dragon

by Holly Stacey

Helgi gazed into the fire and nestled down

into the thick fur rug in front. His grandfather was

snoozing in the wooden chair, his long white beard

mingled with the plate of freshly baked sliced loaf

still sitting, half eaten on his lap.

"Who, wha..." Grandpa woke up with a start,

kicking his left leg and reaching for his belt. "Where's

my sword?" he rumbled.

Helgi giggled. Grandpa often dreamed he was

still adventuring and slaying beasties on the icy seas.

The fact was, it had been many moons since Grandpa

had been on an adventure. The oldest member of the

Viking village meant he was also the best storyteller.

"Go on Grandpa," said Helgi, smiling, "you were

going to tell the story of the Ice Dragon."

Grandpa wriggled in his seat, knocking the bread off his lap. "Huge beastie it was too," said Grandpa. "Larger than any of our dragon ships — at least twice the size! And his icy breath...a frozen death for any who came too close!"

The fire crackled and Grandpa sounded like he was dozing off again, but when Helgi looked closer, he could see the old fire back in his Grandpa's eyes. "I never got close," he said, "but Ari claimed to have sliced one of the scales from its back. Only the very bravest Vikings would seek out the Ice Dragon."

Helgi knew who Ari was — he used to be the blacksmith, now it was his son, Arison, who worked the forge. Ari was legendary among their village as not only wielding fire and sword, but also for being the fiercest warrior.

Later that night Helgi looked out the window of his longhouse and up at the cold winter stars. Somewhere, far up north, the Ice Dragon was probably sleeping in his nest under those same stars. He sighed, pulling the wooden shutter closed, just as a flurry of large snowflakes started to flutter down.

Only the bravest...Helgi hadn't had much chance to be brave yet. He snuggled under his fur-lined blanket and dreamed about finding the Ice Dragon.

It was a frosty morning and Helgi knew what he was going to do. His older brothers were all out at sea with his father and uncles, while he was meant to stay home because he was only eight. Helgi might not have felt brave the first time he went on a Viking adventure (he got seasick), but he was feeling brave now. He packed his bag with shirts and trousers, winter hat and furry mittens, ate his Viking porridge, grabbed some dried fish and bread from the kitchen, and headed out the door.

"Where are you going?" asked Helgi's mum as he left.

"I'm going to find the Ice Dragon and become the bravest Viking in the village."

His mum smiled. "That's nice dear. Make sure you bring back some winter berries while you're out."

And that was that. Helgi nearly raced to the forge — he needed a sword.

"Mornin!" shouted Arison as he squeezed the fire's bellows, causing hot embers to fly about the forge. "What brings you here so early in the day?"

"I'm going to find the Ice Dragon!" Helgi shouted gleefully. "I need a sword!"

Arison stroked his black beard with scarred fingers. "You'll need a very good sword if it's for the Ice Dragon. My father only managed to take a scale from him..." Arison opened a heavy trunk and pulled out a gleaming sword. "Take this," he said. "It has part of the dragon's scale in the hilt and will help protect you on your travels."

Helgi had never seen anything so beautiful. "Th —

thank you! But how can I pay for it?" Everything in

the forge always had a price.

Arison waved his hand casually in the air. "Just

bring me back some more scales — they're worth more

than gold. The sword will be yours."

Helgi took the sword and felt its weight. It

wasn't too heavy and it wasn't too long—the balance

for him was just right. He swished it twice through

the icy air and it made a whistling noise.

Arison chuckled. "See? Looks like you two were

made for each other! Now, off you go to get me more

scales!"

Helgi grinned. But he still had one more place to

visit before he left. The tanner had beautiful hides

that could be turned into shirts, trousers, shoes,

hats, gloves, and sword scabbards.

"Hello?" The tanner's looked dark and empty.

"Is anyone there?" Helgi frowned. The tanner had

probably gone on the sea voyage with most of the

men.

"Yes, come in!" A girl his age was tying

a tanning apron on, but it was twice her size.

Eventually, she gave up and threw it in the corner.

"Anything here you like, just ask. My uncle is out,

but I, Freya, am here to run things while he's gone."

Raising one eyebrow, Helgi looked about the

tanner's shop. Loads of skins were heaped up, already

tanned and ready for cutting. "Do you have any scabbards? I need one for my sword." He pointed to his hip, where the sword was hanging loose off his belt.

The girl's eyes doubled in size. "Is that one of Ari's swords?"

Helgi nodded. "Arison made it. But it has part of the Ice Dragon's scale that Ari brought back."

Freya looked like she was going to faint. Then she bit her lip and looked stern. "Nope, sorry, we don't have any scabbards for that." She half smiled. "However, I could make one for you."

"But I've got to go NOW," said Helgi.

"Take me with you and I can make it on the

way."

Helgi didn't have much to argue with. He needed a scabbard and if having a girl around was the quickest way to get it, then that's the way it had to be. He could send her back before they reached the Ice Dragon. "Done," he finally said, holding out his hand to seal the deal.

She quickly got some things together — tools, leather, food, and a few extra layers. Before Helgi knew it, she was leading the way at a very fast pace.

They travelled for ages, past the boundary of the village, past the farthest pig farm, over the old stone bridge, past the traveler's inn, into the forest and out again. The snowy terrain didn't hinder them or the jutting rocks that came together more frequently as they approached the mountains. Only when the sun started to set did they pause to build a fire and eat.

"My feet hurt," said Helgi, rubbing his toes by the fire. But Freya said nothing. Instead, she pulled out a sheet of leather and started measuring it to fit the sword.

Helgi shrugged and pulled out some bread. "Aren't you hungry?" he asked after he'd eaten and had a drink from his waterskin.

Freya looked up and smiled. "I'll eat when I've finished cutting out the leather."

When the moon had risen higher and the fire died to a low ember, Freya put away her leather and tools and ate supper. Helgi was already fast asleep.

In the morning, Helgi woke to the sound of frying eggs. "Hello!" said Freya cheerfully. She handed him some toasted bread with an egg on it. "There was a bird's nest," she said, pointing, "down there. Dad used to show me how to choose the best eggs. We were fortunate; it's very early for birds to start laying. Don't worry, there are still two left to hatch."

Helgi took the food and frowned. He hadn't expected her to be this useful. But he was determined, when the scabbard was finished, he'd send her home.

They packed up their things and began walking

again. Now the mountain looked much, much bigger

and the snow was deeper, fresher. "Brrr! What an icy

wind!" said Helgi, wrapping himself just a bit tighter.

"Walk faster, it will warm you up." Freya seemed

to be far too cheerful for someone carrying so

much gear. "What will you do when you see the Ice

Dragon?" she asked after a while. The ground was

getting steeper and now they had to climb with their

hands some of the way — holding onto jutting iced-

over rocks. The gear on their backs felt heavier and

Helgi's sword kept scraping the stones. He wished the

scabbard was finished. Just when the climb started to

look too steep for them, it started snowing heavily.

"This way!" shouted Freya. She pointed to

an outcrop of jagged rocks that created a natural shelter from the storm.

The snow came down so fast it looked like a wall of ice. "We may as well stay here," said Helgi, frowning. "By the time it stops, it will be getting too dark to climb anyway." But Freya was already putting dried twigs in a circle. Before she could strike flint and steel, Helgi jumped in and made the spark. For the first time since they set out, he was glad of the company.

The fire warmed their little shelter and as Helgi pulled out his dried fish, Freya continued to work on the scabbard. "There," she said, handing him the finished item. "Try that with the sword." He did, and it was perfect. Smiling, he hooked it onto his belt.

"Now it won't be bashed by the rocks!" she said with
a half-smile.

Snow raged harder and the ground began to
shake. Helgi and Freya looked at each other. They
knew they were close to the Ice Dragon. They had no
idea just how close.

"Quick! Put the fire out!" shouted Helgi. They
gathered the snow and heaped it over the flames,
smothering it quickly. In a flash, the snow cleared and
they saw a white form glide past them in the air. Its
wings were half the length of the village; its claws
were as long as Helgi's sword. Suddenly, finding the
Ice Dragon didn't seem like a very good idea.

"It's so...so...beautiful!" Freya was gazing up at the sky where the dragon had been, an odd look in her eye. "Did you see? It went that way...to those caves."

Helgi had to admit it was a sight to behold. He steeled himself. He'd come all this way to seek out the Ice Dragon, and that was what he'd do. He put his hand over the dragon scale hilt and felt reassured. He no longer wanted to fight it. That would have been madness. Instead, he just wanted to seek it out. Maybe gather some scales to pay for his sword.

"This way! This way!" repeated Freya, tugging at his arm. "Leave the supplies. We'll come back for them. It's only a three hour walk at most. C'mon!"

She half dragged him, half shoved him out of the shelter and into the fresh snow. "Look! It's even closer than it looked!"

Helgi bit his lip and followed Freya. There was some sort of path that made it easier to walk — doubtless carved out from many eager Viking children ready to find the Ice Dragon of legend. How many, he wondered, actually made it home? His bed was sounding pretty nice right now.

Before long, they were at the mouth of a cave littered with shining scales. "This is it!" shouted Freya. "We're rich!"

"Freya, shhhhh!"

But it was too late. The Ice Dragon had heard

them. In seconds, the ground was shaking with his enormous claws. Helgi looked around, but escape was impossible. They would be caught in his frozen breath and trapped in ice forever.

"Who comes to my cave?" boomed the voice of the Ice Dragon.

"Freya the Tanner's Daughter and Helgi the Brave," said Freya boldly. The Ice Dragon loomed over them, making them shake in their boots. He lowered his massive head and looked with frosty eyes at the two children.

"What brings you to my cave, Freya the Tanner's Daughter and Helgi the Brave?"

Freya's eyes glazed over and with a dreamy smile

she said, "Your magnificent scales, Ice Dragon. Only the ones you don't want."

The dragon laughed deeply and the cave rumbled. Helgi gripped his sword by the hilt and stepped in front of Freya to protect her from the dragon's jaws.

"And what's this?" asked the Ice Dragon, taking a closer look at Helgi's sword. "My old scale given to my friend Ari. Well, well, that is interesting." The dragon then sat and looked at the two. "Take my scales, my brave little friends, but you must give me something in return."

This time, Helgi spoke up. "What is that, great dragon?"

"You must tell the most wonderful and

adventurous stories about me. I want every Viking

child quaking in their beds. Only the bravest must

seek me out and only the bravest may have my

scales. Now go, children, and remember your task!"

Together, Freya and Helgi returned home. In the

end they only took three scales each — it was all

they needed. They talked constantly of what stories

they would tell and just before they reached the

Viking village, Helgi remembered to gather some

winter berries for his mother. Even the bravest of

Vikings listened to their mothers.

Spencer, the Very Special Dragon

by Carolyn Findlay Davis

Spencer was a dragon, but not just any old

dragon, as dragons go. Spencer was special. Not

special in just any ordinary way, either. He was as

tall as an old oak tree. He was as wide as a bridge

over a muddy river. His tail was as long as a train

and his eyes were as sparkling as the stars on a dark

night. His scales were brilliant and shiny. When the

sun shone on him he left crystal rainbows all over

the sky. He could breathe fire farther than any of his

friends and you knew that Spencer was around when

you saw the smoke coming from the grass surrounding

the village. Spencer was a dragon, all right. He could

do everything all the other dragons could do. He just

couldn't fly.

Spencer's village was full of dragons. They could

all fly high and had wide glossy wings with gold

scales and pointed edges. They flapped their wings to carry them up and then spread them out as wide as they could to soar on the air currents. The sky was full of dragons over Spencer's village. All day they flew up and down, bumping into each other and blowing out puffs of smoke that looked like white clouds scattered all over the blue sky. But not Spencer.

He walked like an elephant through the tall grass. Stomp, stomp, stomp! He hopped like a kangaroo over the dry land. Hop, hop, hop! He jumped like a frog from one lily pad to another. Thump, thump, thump! He crawled like a worm in the rain. Wriggle, wriggle, wriggle! And he ran as fast as a gazelle running from the lion. Whish, whish, whish! But he couldn't fly.

Spencer tried everything he could think of to help him fly. He jumped off the top of a ladder and fell to the ground. Crash! He jumped out of a swing and flew down to the ground. Squish! He asked his dragon friends to help him, but they were too busy flying around and making cloud pictures with their smoky breath.

One day, Spencer was tired of trying to fly and he squeezed through the neighbor's barn door to see what was inside. It was dark in there and the sunlight couldn't light up his scales. It was small in there so he couldn't jump up and down like a kangaroo. There were strange things in the barn that Spencer hadn't seen before.

Slenderalla the spider was in the corner, spinning a web to catch her dinner. She offered to teach Spencer how to spin a web and said she would share her meal, but he wasn't hungry and, anyway, he just wanted to fly.

Sullivan the black barn snake was hiding under some hay. He offered to show Spencer how to slither under the door, but Spencer couldn't find room to lie down and, anyway, he just wanted to fly.

Winston the cat who ruled the barnyard was busy hunting mice. He offered to show Spencer how to pounce, but Spencer's tail was too long and wide to pounce around inside the barn and, anyway, he just wanted to fly.

"Can anyone teach me to fly?" Spencer asked,

looking around.

Peter the old work horse was standing in his

stall, munching oats, listening to the barn creatures

trying to teach Spencer to do all kinds of things.

Thoughtfully, he looked up. "I have an idea," he said.

"If you come back here tonight I have some friends

who might be able to help you."

Spencer squeezed back out the barn door, not

certain he wanted to come back in the dark. Dragons

weren't afraid of much, but they were afraid of the

dark. None of Spencer's friends came out at night.

Furthermore, if he wanted to fit back through the

door again he would have to skip supper and he knew

tonight was his favorite meal; his mother was cooking

boiled parsnips with radish sauce. That always helped

him breathe out enormous golden puffs of flame. He

thought about it carefully all the way home.

Spencer wanted to fly more than anything. He

wanted to fly more than he wanted boiled parsnips

with radish sauce; he wanted to fly more than he was

afraid of the dark. He just wanted to fly. He didn't

care about anything else.

That night, Spencer crept back to the barn and

squeezed through the door. There were shadows all

around.

Sullivan was hanging from the rafters. "Hiss, hiss,

hiss."

Winston's yellow eyes glowed in the dark. "Meow, meow, meow."

Slenderella was busy munching on her latest catch in her web. "Crunch, crunch, crunch."

Black shadows were flying back and forth around Spencer's head. Swish, swish, swish! He wanted to breathe out his flames to light up the barn but he was afraid he would burn it down.

"So, you're back," Peter said, flicking his tail around up over his back. "Let me introduce you to my buddies here," he said, watching the black shadows flying around the hayloft.

"What are you?" Spencer asked, ducking his

knobby, round head as the black shadows zoomed around him.

"We're bats," squeaked one of the largest shadows as it hovered, looking into Spencer's piercing eyes. "We fly around all night. Do you want to fly with us?"

"I can't fly, that's why I'm here," Spencer said, hanging his head.

"We can't breathe fire, but we can fly. Can you squeeze out the door into the barnyard?" one of the shadows asked.

"Meet you outside," Spencer said, sucking in his rotund tummy and backing out slowly, careful to keep his wide curly tail straight so it wouldn't break the barn door.

Outside, the shadows took shape and Spencer saw the friendly bats spreading their wings and stretching out their legs. They circled around both sides of Spencer and lifted him up, holding onto his scales with their hind legs. "How's that?" More bats latched onto Spencer's tail.

"Wheee! I'm flying!" Spencer let out his breath and great flames shot out ahead, lighting up the sky as more and more bats circled under him. They hung onto his tail and rode on his head. They carried him up and over all the houses in the village. There were no other dragons to get in the way. It was dark!

Spencer's dragon friends looked out their

windows. They had never seen anything so fierce. It looked like a black sky giant with tiny flapping wings and the longest tail they had ever seen. The giant was covered with black moving scales and the fire coming out of its mouth was enough to set the whole town ablaze.

"That was the best night we've had in a long time, Spencer," said one of the bats as they landed in the barnyard. "Let's do it again."

Spencer didn't have to stop eating his boiled parsnips and radish sauce since he didn't have to squeeze into the barn again. The more he ate the brighter his flames grew. He met his new friends in the barnyard every night. He didn't have to try any longer. He was flying.

Spencer listened to his dragon friends telling

stories about the great monster that flew in the night

sky, and he just smiled to himself as he licked radish

sauce off his mouth.

During the day, Spencer walked like an elephant.

He hopped like a kangaroo. He jumped like a frog

and he ran like a gazelle. At night he soared through

the sky with tiny black wings flapping all over his

scales and he breathed out flames of fire to light the

darkness.

Spencer was still a very unique, exceptional, very

special dragon. He could do a lot of things and had a

lot of friends. But, best of all, he could fly!

Magnificent Maude

by Tracey Glasspool

Princess Maude lived with her mother and father,

the Queen and King. She was very clever, very

pretty and very funny. But she was also very bossy,

very demanding and she had very bad manners. She

wanted everything to be magnificent - nothing else

was good enough.

"I want a cake," she said to the Baker. "Make it

magnificent!"

So the Baker baked a delicious strawberry cake

and...

"Lovely!" said everyone.

"Not good enough!" said Princess Maude. "Do it

again."

So the Baker worked all day and made a

scrumptious strawberry and chocolate cake and...

"Wonderful!" said everyone.

"Still not good enough!" said Princess Maude.

"Do it again."

So the Baker stirred and whisked and mixed all day and all night until she had baked a glorious strawberry, chocolate and raspberry cake, covered with whipped cream and marzipan and honeycomb chunks and...

"MAGNIFICENT!" said Princess Maude.

"I want some flowers," Princess Maude said to the florist. "Make them magnificent!"

So the Florist arranged some pretty yellow roses and...

"Lovely!" said everyone.

"Not good enough!" said Princess Maude. "Do it again."

So the Florist worked all day, arranging some

beautiful yellow roses and white lilies and...

"Wonderful!" said everyone.

"Still not good enough!" said Princess Maude.

"Do it again."

So the Florist trimmed and picked and pruned all

day and all night until he had arranged some stunning

yellow roses, white lilies and orange tulips with

feathery green leaves, bright red berries and glittery

twigs and...

"MAGNIFICENT!" said Princess Maude.

"I want a dress," Princess Maude said to the

Dressmaker. "Make it magnificent!"

So the Dressmaker made a dazzling pink satin

dress and...

"Lovely!" said everyone.

"Not good enough!" said Princess Maude. "Do it
again."

So the Dressmaker worked all day and made an

amazing pink satin and cream silk dress and...

"Wonderful!" said everyone.

"Still not good enough!" said Princess Maude.

"Do it again."

So the Dressmaker snipped and pinned and

stitched all day and all night until she had made

a spectacular pink satin, cream silk and white lace

dress covered with sequins and pearls and feathers

and...

"MAGNIFICENT!" said Princess Maude.

It was the day before Princess Maude's birthday.

"I must have a party." said Princess Maude.

"Fetch the Baker, the Florist and the Dressmaker."

But the Baker now screamed every time she

saw an egg and wasn't allowed anywhere near the

royal kitchens. The Florist started sneezing and

wheezing whenever he saw a flower and wasn't

allowed anywhere near the royal gardens. And the

Dressmaker was twitching so badly she definitely

wasn't allowed anywhere near the royal scissors.

"Bother!" said Princess Maude.

"Well," she said, "I shall have to do it myself.

After all, how difficult can it be?"

But, even though Princess Maude spent all day

and all night mixing and whisking, pruning and picking,

pinning and stitching...

Her cake exploded all over the kitchen. Her

flowers made the castle look like a compost heap.

And as for her dress —

"Why are you wearing the curtains dear?" asked

the Queen.

Princess Maude's birthday party was a complete

DISASTER!

"I'm sorry," said Princess Maude in a tiny voice.

"I had no idea how difficult everything was. Or

how hard everyone worked."

Then she clapped her hands.

"I will hold a party for the Baker, the Florist and the Dressmaker — to show them all how sorry I am," she said.

The Queen went pale.

"Are you sure dear?" she said.

"Well," said Princess Maude, "perhaps I might need a little help?"

The Queen smiled, and with everyone's help the party was soon ready. The three guests of honour were brought in...

The Baker (who whimpered ever so quietly when she saw the delicious freshly baked cake), the Florist (who blew his nose ever so gently when he saw the beautifully arranged flowers), and the Dressmaker (who twitched ever so slightly when she saw the

pretty new dress).

"I am very sorry," said Princess Maude. "I didn't

realise how clever you all are." She looked around.

"I promise," she continued, "never to be so fussy

again!"

And everyone, even the Baker, the Florist and the

Dressmaker, clapped and cheered.

"Princess Maude," they all shouted, "you are ...

MAGNIFICENT!"

Princess Pavlova

by Christine Marie Alemshah

DO-DEE-DO! The trumpets sounded. Princess Pavlova had arrived at her new castle.

Duffy Dinosaur peeked his nose out of his mud pit. "Finally, a new neighbor! I hope we can be friends!"

Princess Pavlova peered out from her high tower toward Duffy. "Hmm... he looks friendly. With all this moving, I really could use a new friend."

On Monday, Pavlova decided to invite Duffy over for a tea party. But he did not have proper tea party manners.

"MORE TEA!" yelled Duffy.

Then, he broke her favorite tea cup—CRASH!

And stepped on her train—STOMP! And got dirt in

her sugar jar—SCRUNCH! Pavlova firmly disapproved.

On Tuesday, Duffy invited Pavlova to play in

his mud pit instead. But she had atrocious mud-pit

manners.

"Let's play clean the mud pit," said Pavlova.

Then, she lost his favorite race car in the mud—

SQUISH! And painted all his rocks pink—SWISH!

And sang opera to his venus fly trap—Mi Mi Mi!

Duffy was roaringly mad.

On Wednesday, Pavlova and Duffy decided it was

probably best to meet somewhere in the middle.

"Things will be better at the park," said Pavlova.

"I think so, too," said Duffy.

This time things started off right. Duffy pushed Pavlova on the swing. Then Pavlova let Duffy go first on the slide. They said 'please' and 'thank you' and gave each other high-fives.

By lunch time, things were going so swimmingly they decided to give each other a special surprise.

Pavlova coated Duffy's pterodactyl snack with pink frosting and rainbow sprinkles.

"Ick! My lunch is RUINED!" said Duffy.

Duffy mixed green slime and flies into Pavlova's chef salad.

"I can't eat THIS!" said Pavlova.

"Grr...Park day is t-rex-terminated!" yelled Duffy.

"I royally agree!" echoed Pavlova.

And they both left the park in a huff.

On Thursday, Pavlova and Duffy decided not to play together at all. But as the day wore on, all the things they normally found to be the most fun were no fun at all.

"I had fun in my mud pit before, why is it so boring now?" asked Duffy.

"Humph...Tea service for one is very dull!" said Pavlova.

On Friday, Duffy couldn't stand it any longer. He

snuck over to Pavlova's castle and watched her dance

like a ballerina.

"I wish we were still friends. Then I could

breakdance with her."

Later that morning, Pavlova grew tired of drinking

tea all by herself. So she snuck over and watched

Duffy blowing mud bubbles.

"I wish we were still friends. Then I could make

mud pies with him."

Without knowing what the other was planning,

Pavlova and Duffy both set off for the park. They

arrived to find the other one waiting for them. They

even shared a hug.

"I hoped you would come!" said Duffy.

"Me too," said Pavlova.

"Friends?" asked Duffy.

"Happily and forever after," said Pavlova.

"Wanna breakdance?" asked Duffy.

"Sure!" said Pavlova. "Only after we make some

mud pies."

Kell

by Kai Strand

Keen and cunning, Kell was the best dragon

hoarder around. Her cave was packed full of the

bounty she had pilfered from earls and dukes and

perhaps a king or three. Her favorite targets were

castles because they held the most gleaming gold

and shiny silver under their wooden roofs. Kell soared

high in the air in wide lazy circles, observing the

comings and goings of the castle's occupants until

she learned the best time to attack. Then she would

tuck her leathery wings close to her body and dive

out of the sky like a shooting star. She'd cough a

fireball onto the roof and watch the sun-dried tinder

ignite. In the short amount of time it took for her

to land on a nearby rampart, the castle's occupants

would be scurrying into the courtyard below to

escape the collapsing roof. From that point it was a

simple matter of her picking through the flames to

find the shiniest and prettiest objects to add to her

collection.

One day, Kell tossed aside a heavy wooden beam

that used to support the roof over a throne room.

The flames devouring the room reflected prettily in

the gold of the larger of two thrones. Kell paused

to admire the glittering light but knew she did not

want another throne. Turning away, she spotted a sculpture hanging on a wall. She froze in awe of the sight before her. A large sun stretched from ceiling to floor. The center was a large polished brass circle that gleamed much like the real sun in the surrounding firelight. But what she could not look away from were the sun's rays. They extended out from the shiny center in all directions as if bathing the room in their warmth. But they were made from a metal Kell had never seen before. It had the same reddish brown gleam as her scales. The color of fire and earth mixed in one.

Stomping across the room, she grasped the sculpture and lifted it from the wall. It was taller than her and heavy. She stumbled backward under its weight and hefted the sculpture overhead. Her arms already ached, and she wondered if she could fly all the way home carrying it?

Commotion outside the room alerted her it was time to leave. She looked overhead to see if there was enough room for her to fly with her over-sized package. Though most of the ceiling had burned away, a few large beams remained aflame above her head, effectively blocking her if she were to try to leave with the sun. Glancing over her scale-covered shoulder to make sure the castle guard hadn't made it into the room yet, Kell carefully set the sun down, leaning it against a wall. With a couple flaps of her large wings, she flew high enough to clutch her

arms around a fire-damaged beam and yank it out of

its brackets. Tossing it aside, she flew to the next

beam and did the same. A torrent of shake shingles

and planks, all afire, showered down into the room.

Kell squinted through the thick smoke to see if her

sculpture was damaged. It seemed to wink and blink

happily up at her.

Hurrying, Kell landed heavily on the floor next

to her beloved prize. Tables and walls shook at the

impact of her weight on the floor. A surprised cry

from the crowd sounded like they were just outside

the door. Again, she hefted the sun overhead and

then pumped her wings to lift skyward. The door

flung open before she'd cleared the room. Shouts

and screams could be heard over the crack and hiss

of the fire. Kell flapped as hard as she could to get

out of the castle. Just before she lifted up over the

wall, pain lanced through her wing. She roared, but

managed to continue her escape and soon soared over

the surrounding green pastures dotted with fuzzy

white sheep.

She knew she wouldn't be able to fly for long

with the tear in her wing. Especially carrying such a

large burden. Spotting a stand of trees growing in

a small valley, she crashed clumsily to the ground

just outside them. Panting from the effort of flying,

Kell tromped into the woods. She had to maneuver

the sun up and down and sideways to skirt between tree trunks and under low hanging branches. Her arms shook from exhaustion. A large boulder nestled into a hill presented a good place for her to set her treasure while she rested. She curled up on the soft mound of moss in front of the sun and fell asleep.

When she awoke, the light filtering through the trees had dimmed, and the air was touched with the chill of evening. A dull throb reminded Kell that she needed to attend to her wing. She stood stiffly and stretched her aching muscles. Her arms were the most sore. Rubbing a bicep, she admired how the copper beams of her treasure seemed alive with glowing embers even in the dimming light of evening.

She held her arm out next to a glinting reddish ray and marveled at the sameness of color. The pain was worth it. She would not consider leaving her treasure behind, no matter how much of a challenge transporting it posed.

Kell set off downhill in search of a stream or pond, rolling the sculpture beside her. She smelled the clean water of a brook before she saw it. Fresh water gurgled and skipped over a stony bed. She leaned her sun against a clump of trees and squatted with her toes in the cold flow to wash her wound. First she scooped a paw full of water and sipped it greedily. Then she gently washed the dried blood from the torn edges of her injury. Her wing would heal;

she had many other scars to prove how resilient they
were, but she would be grounded until it did. Based
on the length of the tear, she estimated she would be
stuck in the valley for three days.

She sat on her haunches and peered around the
small valley. Only a small clearing of trees ran along
the erratic path of the brook, which would allow some
sun in but not much. It was important for her to soak
up a lot of sunshine to keep her internal fire stoked.
She peered up at the thin slice of night sky, and a
low worried growl escaped.

An odd squeaky cry caught her attention. It was
followed by coughs and sniffs and other strange
noises that she'd mistaken as part of the babbling

brook. Keeping her serpentine body low to the ground, Kell crept on all fours toward the hiccupping and gasping. She stepped over the brook so as not to make a splashing sound to avoid alerting whatever made the peculiar racket. Slowly and carefully she climbed a small rock pile and peered over the top.

Bright blue eyes as round as coins stared up at her. Tiny rivulets of water leaked out of the eyes and down the face of a girl.

"Don't eat me, please," the girl gasped. Her body shivered, from fear or the cold, Kell was not sure.

"Why would I eat you?" Kell eyed the skinny arms, her gaze stopping on the awkward angle of the girl's left ankle. "You're hurt."

The girl blinked and shivered and finally nodded.

"Let me help you." Kell crawled over the top of

the rock pile and down the other side.

The girl squeaked again and scooted backward,

wincing when her hurt ankle bumped against a rock.

"For fire's sake, I'm not going to hurt you," Kell

said and tromped toward the girl, sending showers of

river rock skittering down the pile as she progressed.

Lifting the girl in her arms, Kell carried her up

and over the rock pile to where the sun sculpture

rested against the tree. The girl's eyes grew even

larger when she saw it. Setting the girl down gently,

Kell scoured the ground to find two sturdy branches

and some green vines.

"This is going to hurt," Kell warned. As carefully

as possible, she set the thick straight branches on

either side of the girl's ankle and then tied them

together with the vines. As she tightened the vine,

the ankle straightened. The girl gnawed her lip and

dug her fingers into the earth but didn't cry out.

Kell built a fire, lighting the tinder with one

of the last puffs from her gullet. She would need

to soak up a lot of sun the next day to refill her

reserves. She gathered berries from the woods and

shared them with the girl. "It isn't much. I'll hunt

tomorrow." Curling up next to the girl, she peered at

her from one eye. "Goodnight."

The next morning Kell was devastated to wake

to drizzle. She hurried to find plenty of dried fallen branches to keep the fire going. Kell wasn't sure she had enough fire inside her to start a new blaze if it were to go out. She saw the girl curled up in a small ball, shivering, and realized she had to protect her from the rain. Kell eyed her sculpture, her heart already breaking over what she knew she had to do.

Bending the pretty copper rays at a 90-degree angle, Kell created a shelter. The large brass disk was a perfect ceiling against the rain and the bent rays acted as strong walls that helped to keep the heat in. Because the rays tapered to a point, the walls were not solid but that allowed for the smoke from the fire to escape. Kell left a couple rays untouched, and they acted as a doorway.

After their meal of roasted rabbit and more berries, Kell curled up outside the door, happy to see the girl's clothing had dried and she no longer shivered.

"Why are you caring for me?" the girl whispered. "Why don't you leave me and fly away?"

"I'm unable to fly," Kell explained. "My wing is injured." She unfurled her wing to show the tear. It was already knitting up nicely and was significantly shorter than it had been the day before.

"Did you hurt the people?" the girl's voice was barely audible. "At the castle. Did you hurt them?"

Kell frowned. "What castle?"

The girl lifted her gaze to the brass disk above her. "Where you got this."

The dragon's heart lurched unexpectedly. She could see the girl was afraid of the answer, but needed to ask. "I never hurt the people. Why didn't you say something yesterday when you recognized the sculpture?"

Relief mixed with the fear that never left the girl's expression. "I thought you might make a meal of me and that the answer wouldn't matter."

Two days later, Kell's wing was healed. Cradling the girl in her arms, she flew back to the castle and landed heavily in the courtyard. People screamed and scattered. Guards drew swords and knocked arrows in their bows.

The girl cried out, "Do not hurt the dragon!"

Gasps of horror swelled through the crowd as

though they'd only just realized the dragon held the

girl.

"I will not hurt you," Kell said. "I only want to

return the girl."

Cries and gasps filled the air again. "It speaks!"

The large wooden doors of the castle swung open,

and the queen stumbled forward followed by the king.

"Adele!" the queen cried. She fell to her knees in

front of Kell, and mud seeped into the rich velvet of

her gown. "Please, do not hurt my daughter."

Guards rushed forward to put themselves between

the dragon and their king and queen.

"Stand down," the king called. His gaze lingered

on the makeshift splint on his daughter's ankle. "You

have brought her back to us."

Kell bowed her head and then met the king's

eye. "I am sorry for the destruction I caused. Please

forgive me." She bent forward and laid Adele in the

king's arms.

"Daddy, can I have your medallion, please?"

Adele asked.

The king frowned, but nodded.

Adele lifted it from around his neck and turned

toward Kell. "Can you hold out your wrist, please?"

When she did, Adele slid the chain over her large

scaly hand and let it rest on Kell's wrist like a

bracelet.

Kell spun the chain until the medallion showed,

and she grinned a horrible, toothy grin. A round medal

made of the pretty metal the same color as her

scales hung from the chain. "How did you know?"

"I saw how hard it was for you to sacrifice the

sun for my shelter. You stared at the rays the most,"

Adele said. "I didn't want you to leave without some

copper to take with you."

"Copper? Is that what it is called?" Kell asked,

admiring how the medallion almost disappeared from

view when it lay against her arm. She smiled at

Adele. "Thank you, princess."

"Thank you, dragon, for not hurting my family and for helping me," Adele said. "I hope you will visit again."

Startled by the offer, Kell looked at the king and queen to gauge their reactions.

"As long as you promise to keep our new roof intact," the king said.

"Yes, sir. I won't be pillaging anymore." Kell stared at her copper medallion.

"You won't?" the king asked.

"I've always been careful not to cause physical harm to the inhabitants when I plundered, but Adele made me realize I've been harming them anyway." Kell tapped her chest over her heart. "Here."

"The hoard I have will keep me happy forever.

Especially now." Kell lifted her wrist to indicate her

newest treasure. "I would love to visit in the spring

when the fields are filled with heather and new buds

cover the trees."

"We'd be happy to have you, dragon," the queen

said.

"Kell, please call me Kell." She unfurled her

wings, careful not to hit any of the guards. "Heal

well, Adele. I'll take you for a fly when I visit in the

spring."

Adele's eyes sparkled with the promise.

The king glowered.

Kell lifted skyward. The storm had finally broken

up enough to allow some sun through, and it sparked

like embers from a fire off of Kell's scales as she

flew toward the fluffy white clouds.

Adele shielded her eyes against the glints of

light. From the safety of her father's arms, she waved

until she could no longer see the beast in the sky.

Kingdom of the Dragons

by Amanda Hill

In a high mountain kingdom where dragons made their lairs, there lived a prince who should have been happy. But he was not.

A heavy cloud hung over the kingdom, threatening the lives of all who lived within its borders. The king was frantic. The soldiers so fearful they were deserting. And every villager — down to the tiniest mouse — lived in constant terror.

The dragon Althenia cast her gigantic shadow across field and farm almost daily, her huge purple wings beating against the sky and her unearthly

screech echoing from mountain top to mountain top.

The soldiers' weapons proved useless against her.

Althenia cast them aside like twigs. Then she chased

them back to the castle, breathing fire at their heels.

Some said the dragon was nursing a nest of

hatchlings in her high mountain lair. Babies who would

surely grow into fire breathing adults. It was a dark

time indeed.

The young prince threw open the shutters of

his bedchamber window and looked out across

the kingdom that would someday be his. He was

only thirteen but he already felt the weight of

responsibility. The army had failed to keep the

kingdom safe and would surely fail again. It was time

for him to face his destiny. The dragon, Althenia must

be killed. And Basil knew, as crown prince, he must

do it himself.

His hands shook as he lifted his crown from the

shelf and placed it on his head. Dragons were said to

like such things. Perhaps it would be of some use. He

gulped back his fear and swung out of the window. No

one must see him go.

Following a steep mountain trail, he approached

the dragon's lair as soundlessly as a fox. But a voice

within him screamed, "What are you doing? How

can one defenseless boy defeat a dragon that has

decimated an entire army?"

Basil shook his fear aside and crept into the cave,

feeling his way along the rock wall with his fingers. It

was cold and damp. A putrid smell filled his nostrils

and the whirr of winged creatures circled about him.

"Do not fear," he told himself, but when a wild

screech echoed through the cave, he whipped around

and darted back, as though his legs had a mind of

their own.

On his third step, he found no earth beneath

his feet and fell like a stone dropping from a ledge.

Terror ran through him like a river of ice. He clawed

at the air and kicked with his feet, banging his legs

against the rock wall as he fell.

He screamed out in agony and the sound of his

own voice echoed back to him like the cry of a wild animal. At last he landed with a thud in a pile of sticks and leaves, curled himself into a ball, and sobbed. Every inch of his body ached.

The young prince pushed himself up to sit among the leaves. Through his sobs, he pulled his crown from his tunic and placed it on his head. If he was to end his life as bait for a dragon, he must do it as the prince he was.

The minutes ticked by while he waited for Althenia to swoop him up and crush him with her talons. But she did not come. When his eyes adjusted to the darkness, he realized that he had fallen into a huge nest. A nest in which five eggs, almost as large as himself, lay one next to the other. He imagined the

young dragons hatching and eating him alive.

Scratching and scraping sounds echoed from the

cave entrance. Basil's heart stopped cold. Althenia

was entering her lair. Despite his aching body, he

dove to the eggs and hid himself between them.

Soon, two golden eyes peered down into the

nest. Basil burrowed into the sticks and leaves as

a monstrous nose with flaring nostrils touched the

eggs one by one. Satisfied, the dragon settled her

massive body beside the nest and covered it with one

enormous wing. Very soon she fell asleep.

Basil knew he must escape or be killed by the

dragon. But his bruised body refused to move. There

was nothing he could do but hide among the eggs and hope Althenia would not notice him before she left to hunt at the break of day.

He found it very hard to sleep. His ankle was swollen and throbbed with pain. It must have been past midnight when he felt the egg beside him move. At first he thought he had been dreaming, but when the leathery shell of the egg began to rip, he knew it was no dream. He was about to share the nest with a baby dragon.

Before the hatchling had freed itself from its shell, the other eggs in the nest also began to move. The clawed feet of dragon hatchlings tore at their leathery prisons as they wiggled and squirmed their way into the world. Basil did the only thing he could think to do. He pulled a piece of egg shell over himself and lay very still.

He awoke to the squawking of baby dragons and felt them scrambling about the nest. Peering through a tear in the shell, he saw Althenia's golden eyes. She was awake.

Tenderly, she nudged each baby with her huge nose and snorted softly to them. They responded with snorts and squawks of their own.

Suddenly, Althenia's scaly nose and amber eyes aimed straight for his egg. Basil curled into a ball and closed his eyes. But the egg shell flew off, leaving him completely exposed to her gaze. He dared not move.

Althenia stared and Basil held his breath. Then, to his amazement, she touched his crown with her nose and snorted. Soon she began to nuzzle him in exactly the same way she had done with the hatchlings. "She thinks I'm one of her babies," Basil thought.

The moment she left the cave, Basil crawled to the edge of the nest and searched for some way to escape. Perhaps when his ankle healed he could climb out. But what could he do until then? Pretend to be a baby dragon? At least his fellow hatchlings had not tried to eat him.

It was not long until Althenia returned with

breakfast. The hatchlings devoured the scraps of

meat she fed them without even swallowing, but Basil

could only stare at his. Althenia cocked an eye and

nudged him softly. He pretended to eat for her sake,

but when she looked away he gave it to a grateful

nest mate.

After several missed meals, however, his stomach

began to rumble. Soon he was hungry enough to eat

almost anything. He closed his eyes and swallowed

the raw meat Althenia gave him.

By the fifth day, Basil realized he was beginning

to understand the dragon's speech. What had seemed

like nothing but snorts and squawks, was in fact,

a simple language. A language he soon learned to

imitate.

His ankle grew stronger. He would soon find a way to escape. But what could he tell his father? He had come here to kill this dragon. It was his duty. But he had learned to love the gentle dragon and his innocent nest mates. What could he do?

At last he came to a difficult decision. Althenia may turn him to charcoal with her breath, but he must talk to her. Perhaps, they could find a solution together.

When Althenia brought breakfast the next morning, he didn't eat with the others. Instead he looked up into her golden eyes and touched her gently. Then, using the language he had learned from the hatchlings, he said, "Mother Dragon, may I speak to you?"

Althenia cocked her head, "Speak on, my son."

"I must tell you," he said, "that I am not your son."

Althenia seemed to smile and answered, "Do you think I do not know this?"

Basil's mouth opened in shock. "But you have cared for me and brought me food. Why?"

"I liked the shine on your head. And you were young and injured. I am a mother — so I cared for you."

"But, Mother Dragon," Basil said. "My people are at war with your kind."

Althenia closed her eyes and turned her head to the side. "My kind has not always warred with your kind. Once we lived in peace." She turned back and looked him in the eye. "Now your soldiers kill us and hang our heads in their castles. We do what we must."

"But what if the soldiers did not hunt you?" Basil asked. "Would you leave the people in peace?"

"Yes. Go to your father, human hatchling. Tell him the dragon Althenia does not wish for war. If his soldiers will hunt me no more and allow my hatchlings to mature in peace, I will protect your kingdom from all enemies. Tell him."

Three days later, Basil returned to the castle.

His parents had thought him dead. They were so overjoyed by his return that a great festival was declared in his honor. As the day drew to a close and the sky turned to crimson, a great screech was heard. Then, winging her iridescent body across the scarlet sky, Althenia circled three times before swooping earthward.

The people screamed in terror, overturning tables and spilling food and drink in their haste to get away. The soldiers drew their arrows and took aim. But the King silenced them by raising his arms and lifting his scepter. "Do not fear, my people," he cried out. "This dragon is not a foe, but a friend."

As the soldiers lowered their bows and the people

peered cautiously from behind overturned tables, the

King continued. "This dragon cared for my son as

one of her own. She has proven herself to be gentle

and kind. She proposes a bargain, which we shall

accept. From this day forward we will protect her and

her young and she will protect our kingdom from all

enemies."

Amid a murmuring crowd, the dragon settled

beside the King, folded her wings, and dropped her

head. "Althenia," he said, "we accept your bargain.

You are welcome in our kingdom."

Basil stepped from his father's side and threw

his arms around the dragon's neck. She nuzzled him

toward her lowered wing, and he scrambled up to sit

astride her back.

Althenia spread her wings and lifted skyward. A

cheer went up from the crowd, and the huge dragon

spat fire into the night sky.

From that day to this, there has been peace in

the land protected by the monstrous reptilian beasts.

A land that has become known as - the Kingdom of

the Dragons.

Tinky's Wish

by Julie Sandpiper

Tinky, a fairy princess with soft brown eyes and

dark black curls that tumbled down her back, woke up

in her big bed full of pillows to see snow on the little

round window of her room. She ran to the window

and looked out at all the soft white snow covering

the trees and hills outside her castle. Her white

wings flapped gently, and she wore the loveliest blue

silk nightdress. Today was a special day. Tinky was

turning six. Every fairy princess gets three wishes on

her birthday. Tinky had tossed and turned most of the

night, wondering what to wish for. Once she decided,

she got a few hours' sleep on her pink soft pillow in

her warm bed.

Putting on her most special silver sparkling dress,

and fastening diamond clips in her hair, she went

downstairs to her parents.

"Happy Birthday, Tinky! Are you ready for your

wishes?" her parents, the king and queen fairy,

chorused.

"I'll make my wishes when I blow out the candles

on my birthday cake!" Tinky replied. Her parents

nodded because it seemed like a good time for wishes.

Tinky's party was so much fun. Lots of little boy

and girl fairies attended and lots of animals too!

There was an ice-skating cat, a dancing bear, and a

great big elephant who let Tinky slide down his trunk

just for fun. When the cake came out, it was so big

and covered with so much pink icing it looked like a

cloud from the sky! Six candles stood on the top of the cake.

It was time. All the little fairies, the ice-skating cat, big bear, and great big elephant were quiet, wondering what Tinky would wish for. Tinky blew out the candles.

"I wish I had a new teddy bear!" Immediately, a big, fuzzy, soft blue teddy bear appeared. She hugged it. It was just the right size to keep her company at night and would fit in her bed nicely.

"For my second wish, I would like my parents to have good health all year long!" Tinky really was a kind-hearted and thoughtful fairy. Her mother, a beautiful queen fairy with soft golden curls smiled, and her headache cleared up on the spot.

"And my third wish..." Tinky paused. The fairies listened. The cat, bear, and great big elephant all wondered what she would say. This was her biggest wish. It was something she wanted for a very long time.

"I wish for...a dragon!"

Her parents gasped. Dragons were big, dangerous, noisy, and breathed fire, after all.

"Tinky, no!" her mother cried, but it was too late. On the table next to the lovely pink cake sat a golden, gleaming, giant egg. It was hot to touch.

"Hurrah! My very own dragon." Tinky clapped her hands with joy.

She kept the egg on a satin pillow next to her bed. Every night she stared at the golden egg, waiting for it to hatch. She talked to it, whispered it secrets, and sang it songs.

Every night her parents hoped it wouldn't hatch soon and worked on building a great big pen for the dragon.

One summer day when the sun was strong and all the birds sang songs, a crack appeared on the shell of the golden egg. Crick! Crack! The shell broke open and what did Tinky see?

A tiny blue snout appeared. And then two small yellow eyes. Soon, a whole baby dragon climbed out of the golden egg! He was beautiful with blue wings and a long tail. When he hiccupped, fire shot out of his mouth with a whoosh!

Tinky gently took the dragon in her hands.

"Welcome, dragon! I'm Tinky and you're...Blue. I'm yours and you're mine forever!" she promised, putting him on the satin pillow, which she moved onto her bed. He curled up to sleep, because egg-cracking is difficult work. Tinky ran to the castle library to find her parents studying the monthly report from the fairy kingdom. Her mother wore a beautiful golden dress that matched the color of her curly hair. Her father, whose hair was dark like Tinky's, was in a blue regal robe. They followed Tinky to her bedroom as soon as she told them the news.

"Isn't he adorable?" her mother said, petting the sleeping dragon's back with one finger.

"He is cute, isn't he?" her father agreed. "But look at those sharp teeth." Two fangs poked out of Blue's mouth even though his jaw was closed.

"And he can breathe fire!" Tinky proudly remembered the hiccup.

"What?" her parents chorused.

"He should sleep outside then," her mother said nervously.

"Too dangerous to keep in the house," her father agreed, nodding his head.

"But it was only a little fire that came out. He's so small, he can't do any harm," Tinky pleaded.

Her parents agreed he could sleep on her bed until he got bigger. But they warned her he would soon have to sleep outside in the pen.

Blue was only a little dragon, but even when he was a month old he was able to do the most delightful things. Jumping into the air, he would flap his wings until he was the same height as Tinky, looking into her brown eyes with his yellow ones. He could do a somersault in mid-air. And he liked to light the candles in the castle by breathing on them with his fire. Though this made Tinky clap her hands, her mother would press her hand to her heart and gasp, and her father would shake his head, frowning.

After just two months, Blue was taller and came

up to Tinky's knee. Her parents told her it would

be the last night Blue could sleep on her bed. This

made Tinky sad because she liked to curl up next to

the dragon and see him sleeping on the pillow beside

her. She tried not to cry because it would make Blue

sad, so they counted one hundred stars through the

bedroom window and settled down to sleep.

Before long, a noise boomed through the house.

Crash!

Tinky sat up with her eyes wide, clutching her

blue teddy bear tightly. Blue sniffed the air and

hopped down from his puffy pillow, pattering out of

the room on his little dragon feet. Tinky hesitated.

She wanted to hide in her room under the covers. The

thing that made the noise could be a monster. Or a

burglar. Or something else very bad.

But could she let Blue face the Bad Thing all

alone? She decided she couldn't. Jumping out of her

bed, she ran to the hallway and followed Blue down

the stairs. They hid in the shadows by the kitchen

door.

Thump! The noise came from the kitchen. Bump!

Carefully, Tinky opened the door just partway with

a creak. Peering through the crack, they saw a little

brown bear.

Tinky covered her mouth and gasped. Though it

was just the size of Tinky, the bear had big claws

and powerful teeth. It turned over the cookie jar and

smashed the bread box on the floor. Tinky's favorite

chocolate cookies spread everywhere.

"Tinky! What are you doing out of bed at this

time?" whispered her mother, who had come to see

what the noise was about

"Shh! A bear is in the kitchen," Tinky whispered

back.

"A bear? How did a bear get in the castle?"

her father said. Her parents were both wearing silk

pajamas and had bed head.

"I don't know, but it's there!" Tinky cracked open

the door again, and all of them looked through. Three

pairs of fairy eyes and one pair of dragon eyes stared

into the kitchen through the crack in the door.

"It's a cute little baby bear," her mother

exclaimed as they watched the brown bear dip its paw

into the honey jar.

"Still," her father whispered, "it's big enough and

strong enough to give us nasty cuts with those sharp

claws on its paws and bite us with its teeth."

Tinky agreed. As the baby bear licked the honey

off its paw, she could see that its claws were long

and sharp.

"True," her mother nodded her head, her curls

bouncing. "It's as big as any of us."

Blue just blinked.

They watched the bear eat all the honey, all of

Tinky's favorite chocolate cookies, and the bread.

The little bear gave a loud burp and curled up on the

tiled floor to sleep.

Once the bear started to snore, Blue flapped his

wings and flew silently into the kitchen.

"No, Blue!" Tinky reached out her hands to catch

him, but it was too late.

"Blue, come back!" her parents pleaded. The

little dragon was only the size of the bear's head. He

could get hurt.

But dragons have a lot of magic. Most of it is

secret and only revealed in very dire situations like

this one. Blue began to sing a pretty song.

It had no words, and sounded like, "Ra ra ra ra

ra." As he sang, an amazing thing happened.

The baby bear, eyes closed, got to his feet.

Blue kept singing as he flew to the door. The bear

followed. Tinky opened the door wide with both hands,

and the dragon and bear came into the hallway. Her

father ran to the great castle entrance, undid all the

locks, and pushed the big oak door open so that Blue

could lead the bear out into the forest.

They watched as Blue stopped singing, and the

little bear curled up under a tree, its eyes still

closed. When Blue came back to the house, they were

full of praise.

"You were so brave!" Her mother clapped her

hands.

"Well done!" Her father beamed.

"I knew you could do it!" Tinky hugged Blue.

After that, her parents bought Blue an even

bigger satin pillow to sleep on and often said how it

made them feel safe to have a dragon in the house

and that Tinky's wish was the best one she ever

made.

There's a Dragon in the Library

by Nancy Julien Kopp

....

Wilhemina Higgins' long braids bounced as she ran down the narrow tunnel the bookshelves made in the Westlake Public Library. Her untied shoelaces slapped against well-worn sneakers. Past the Js, Ks, and Ls she flew, slowing only slightly as she rounded the corner.

Her heart thumped when she spied the dragon waiting at the end of the row of shelves. She screeched to a sudden stop.

At first it was silent then the monster snorted a little, lifted its huge head, took a gigantic breath inward and fell silent again.

Wilhemina swallowed and took one step back. Before she could turn and retrace her path, the enormous dragon reared back on its hind legs, threw its massive head backward, and breathed out with a whoosh! Smoke curled from its nostrils, and flames poured forth from the great mouth. The dragon clawed the air and flapped magnificent wings. The green and purple scales that covered the beast from head to toe gleamed under the library lights. Its amber eyes glinted like cut crystal.

"Wilhemina Higgins!" the dragon shouted. "How many times have you been told there is no running in the library?

"Do you mean today, Miss Philpot?" Wilhemina looked right into the dragon's eyes. "Or did you mean all week?"

"You know the rules," the librarian said. "Why do you come here, if not to read?" Miss Philpot breathed heavily, as she opened and closed her claws.

Wilhemina feared she might start snorting and breathing fire again at any minute, but her voice was as firm as Miss Philpot's. "My mother doesn't get home from work until 5 o'clock. She says the library is a safe place for me to stay after school."

The dragon pulled her sweater close around her shoulders. "If you cannot follow the rules, you must go outside."

"It's cold as a bowl of ice cream out there, and it's going to rain, too." Wilhemina answered.

"Then go sit on the steps."

"The steps are hard as rocks."

"You could stay at school," Miss Philpot answered, barely moving her lips as she spoke.

"There's no one there," Wilhemina answered back in the same way, lips scarcely moving.

"Then you must study." Miss Philpot's eyes flashed, and her hands turned claw-like once more.

"I've studied all day," Wilhemina told her. She

folded her arms and spread her feet apart, ready for

battle.

The dragon hissed and narrowed its eyes. "Don't

be insolent."

"I don't know what that means," Wilhemina said.

"Then go look it up!" Miss Philpot cried as she

turned away and moved rapidly to her desk.

Wilhemina felt a tug on her shirt tail. "What do

you want?"

Eyes wide, the culprit looked up at Wilhemina. "Is

she mad at you?"

Wilhemina sighed. "Every day. So, what's your

problem, Lucy Ann?"

"I'm bored."

"Then go read a book." Wilhemina thought her answer sounded a great deal like Miss Philpot.

"Can't read yet," Lucy Ann replied. She pushed her bottom lip over the top one and stared at Wilhemina.

"Oh go away and leave me alone," Wilhemina said. She walked quickly along the line of shelves ignoring the brightly colored book jackets she passed. She stopped at the tall library windows where rain beat against the panes and thunder made them rattle. She put her elbows on the windowsill, curled her hands around her cheeks, and watched the wind bend the tree branches outside.

There was another tug on her shirt. Without

looking around, she said, "What do you want now,

Lucy Ann?"

"Read this to me," Lucy Ann said, holding up a

large picture book.

Wilhemina accepted the book Lucy Ann held out.

"Why not?"

They marched past the dragon's desk. Miss

Philpot watched silently, but Wilhemina thought she

could see tiny wisps of smoke curling from under her

nose.

The two girls sat at a round table, and Wilhemina

read aloud in a quiet voice, wriggling on her chair as

she turned the pages.

"You can do better than that, Wilhemina." Lucy

Ann scowled. "You sound dull."

There was a moment of silence. Then Wilhemina said, "You're right!" She sat up straighter, flipped back to page one, and read with more feeling. She used a different voice for each character in the story. Halfway through, she noticed three more listeners around the table.

"Go on," one of them said when she stopped reading.

Wilhemina laughed and continued reading the story and showing the pictures to the younger children.

From the corner of her eye, she spied a fluffy, long-haired cat. Its amber eyes surveyed the group at the table as it danced about on dainty paws. The cat

purred deep in its throat.

When Wilhemina closed the book, the cat purred

again said, "Wilhemina Higgins, you read that book

most wonderfully well. Perhaps you could start an

after-school story club. What do you think?"

"I think I would like that very much, Miss

Philpot." Wilhemina reached out to shake the paw the

librarian offered her.

Register:

Register on our website (www.knowonder.com/register) to get **FREE** access to over 500 orignal stories, education tools and other resources to help you give the gift of literacy to your child, each and every day.

About Us:

Knowonder is a leading publisher of engaging, daily content that drives literacy; the most important factor in a child's success.

Parents and educators use Knowonder tools and content to promote reading, creativity, and thinking skills in children from zero to twelve.

Knowonder's Literacy Program – delivered through storybook collections – delivers original, compelling new stories every day, creating an opportunity for parents to connect to their children in ways that significantly improve their children's success.

Ultimately, Knowonder's mission is to eradicate illiteracy and improve education success through content that is affordable, accessible, and effective.

Learn more at

www.knowonder.com

Printed in Great Britain
by Amazon.co.uk, Ltd.,
Marston Gate.